W9-BLI-670

Teddy and the Mudblups

This story shows the value of using
your imagination and the value of being neat.

Story by:
Ken Forsse

Illustrated by:
David High
Russell Hicks
Rennie Rau
Theresa Mazurek

WORLDS OF WONDER™

© 1985 Alchemy II, Inc. "Patents Pending." All rights reserved. Worlds of Wonder is the exclusive licensee, manufacturer and distributor of the World of Teddy Ruxpin toys. "Teddy Ruxpin," "Grubby," "Fobs," "Newton Gimmick," "Mudblups" and "World of Grundo" are trademarks of Alchemy II, Inc., Northridge, CA. "A Friend for Life has Come to Life" and the symbol W•W are trademarks of Worlds of Wonder, Inc., Fremont, California.

Grubby™
Newton Gimmick™
Princess Aruzia™
Leota™
Wooly What's-It™
Prince Arin™
Fobs™

Page 1

Grubby and Gimmick stopped being upset with each other and we took off in the Airship.

We flew the Airship to the edge of the Great Desert.

Gimmick's idea did work very well. We were able to turn the Airship into a house.

We all took mud and
smeared it on ourselves.

We made it back to the Airship.